PRAISE FOR WRESTLING ALONG THE WAY

I love the heart of this book! I love the fact that Stephen boldly, humbly, and honestly addresses topics and questions in scripture and in the church that many of us wrestle with in our search for truth. At the heart of each chapter is Jesus' love and humility seasoned with some good humor along the way. As I read this book, I found myself wiping away tears of joy thinking about loving, healthy, thoughtful discussions around the things of God where relationships with one another grow instead of divide.

Searching for the truth, learning how to listen better to God's voice, and seeking first His Kingdom together is at the heart of this book. We definitely will be wrestling along the way, but Jesus promises that if we seek, we will find. This book will help you go deeper with Jesus – the way, the truth and the life, and will challenge you as you continue your search for His truth with grace and love.

— PASTOR DARLENE FRANKS,
OROVILLE CA CHURCH OF THE
NAZARENE

It is often said that the two topics to avoid at a family gathering are politics and religion. While that might be sage advice for getting along for the holidays, there certainly is a time to have these conversations. In a time when the art of good conversation has been lost in many ways, Stephen transparently invites us into a truly refining process of wrestling through some of the tougher questions in regards to faith. Read a chapter, set the book down, and use the follow-up questions to wrestle with these subjects yourself. Better yet, grab a cup of coffee with a peer and take this journey together.

— PASTOR MATTHEW GARNER,
SUTTER CREEK CA CHURCH OF THE
NAZARENE

I have known Stephen Lindsey for almost 40 years, and have observed him to be an analytical thinker, always asking the probing questions while firmly committed to the Christian faith. In this little volume Steve writes from the heart, sharing his faith journey while exposing his own struggles about what it means to follow The Way. Hoping to stimulate discussion around important issues, he prods the reader to ponder one's own faith. The questions at the conclusion of each chapter will undoubtedly stimulate indepth sharing among searching thinkers. I highly commend this book for use in small prayerful group settings where participants are willing to listen to one another as they seek to walk the path of faithful discipleship together.

— DR. KEN HEFLIN, UNITED
METHODIST PASTOR

If you are looking for answers, you won't find them in this book. Instead, this work will spark in you a newfound curiosity and desire to dig deep in the exploration of your Christian faith and the questions that inherently come with it. This thought-provoking work reads just like you're having an honest conversation with a trusted friend. Whether you're a long-time Jesus follower or a brand-new believer, walk with Steve and discover that even as we wrestle with big questions, we have a God who lovingly provides us with both His definitive truth and His unending grace.

— PASTOR AUSTIN BENDER, SUTTER CREEK CA CHURCH OF THE NAZARENE

This book is dedicated to all those followers of the Way who courageously seek relationship with God beyond the superficial.

WRESTLING ALONG THE WAY

A Journey in Christian Faith

STEPHEN LINDSEY

Lindsey Enterprises Inc.

CONTENTS

Jesus said, "I am the way, the truth, and the life. No one comes to the Father except through me."

— JOHN 14:6

PREFACE

My intent in writing this book is to share with fellow Christians, followers of the Way, what I and others have wrestled with in our search for truth. It is important, or more accurately, it is imperative that we anchor our faith in truth. It seems there is a growing trend in churches and our society in general to accept the assertions of others without question, without research, without pondering and without seeking the confirmation of that still, small voice inside of us.

I am not an expert. I have no degree in theology or other credentials. Having been a Christian for nearly fifty years, I continue to be the student, not the professor. I used to know just enough to be dangerous. As I have continued to learn more, I know that I don't know very much.

Just as the sport of wrestling can test a person's physical and mental limits, so is the challenge to navigate life in the face of good and evil, selfishness and service, pain and pleasure, good times and bad times. This little book will generate more questions than answers. Perhaps it will spark an interest in seeking life and truth beyond our daily existence.

My hope is that those who read these pages will be fellow searchers along the Way, searching for truth and meaning in their lives. Further, that their discussions with each other will be open, honest, and tolerant of those who might have a different understanding, a different interpretation. On the other hand, my fear is that this book will generate arguments, divisiveness, judgment, and condemnation. Little good will come from that.

May we model how we interact with each other the way Jesus interacts with us. May we become more in alignment with His will and teachings as we wrestle with life's challenges. Sanctify us, oh Lord, in our journey.

WALKING WOUNDED

In elementary school, I stood on the playground with several boys comparing our scars. It was a big deal to have the best scar and there was real status in coming to school with your arm in a cast. Somehow, these trophies of past battles were revered like medals of honor. A good scar confirmed that one was a warrior in the struggles of childhood. As an adult, I've accumulated a couple of scars that I would have been proud to display on the elementary playground with my buddies.

The term "walking wounded" became common during the early 1900's, usually referring to soldiers in war time or victims of natural disasters. It referred to those who had been hurt, but not so badly that they could not function. Since then, the term has been expanded to include psychological or emotional dysfunction where the wounded person can continue to function in daily life. Though not readily visible, emotional scars can go deep. Some of us with horrific scars appear totally fine on the outside.

Who among us does not carry emotional scars? Who has gone through life unscathed? For example, I know of no one who claims to have had perfect parents. There is no requirement that we take parenting classes before becoming one. Even those of us who vow to do a better job of parenting than we ourselves received manage to mess things up. Worse is the parent that is so dysfunctional as to not have the capacity to meet their children's needs. Even worse than that is the parent who is so messed up as to deliberately abuse and mistreat the ones that they should love the most.

In addition to imperfect parenting, many of us have been hurt by others, from the school playground to the career workplace. Who has never been rejected by peers? Who has never been betrayed by a close friend or romantic interest? What marriage that has gone beyond the honeymoon stage has never experienced conflict, fights, or even out and out warfare? We have all been hurt by others in one way or another. We have all been the recipients of lies, theft, and ridicule. As a teenager, I once got beat up because I was in the wrong place at the wrong time, and my skin was the wrong color. My assailant was an angry young man looking for someone on whom he could release his furry. That one was really nothing personal; anyone would do.

The wounds that hurt the most and go the deepest come from people we trust, those we let on the inside, those we love. We are speaking here of family, spouses, close friends, and workplace friends that we rely and depend on for unity. Sticks and stones may break bones, but words can pierce the heart. In church families, we tend to let our guard down because we expect fellow members to be kind and caring. A scratch on our car door from a careless stranger in the parking lot does not hurt as badly as an unkind or cutting comment from someone we trust. It's going to happen. We are imperfect people living in a world full of other imperfect people.

When hurt, we either withdraw or lash back at the source of our pain. It is completely natural to defend ourselves, in fact, it is survival. Yet, at the same time, we were designed to be in relationship with others. If we withdraw too far, the result can be crippling. If we lash back in excess, we become worse than the "enemy" we are fighting against. Who has never reacted too severely and hurt someone else? How many of us wish we had thought things through before saying something we soon regret? Anyone who claims to have no regrets in life is either lying, ignorant, or has advanced dementia.

And, so we go on. We continue to have relationships. We struggle to get it right and make things better. We continue to mess up on occasion, hopefully not as frequently or severely as in the past. We don't move to the arctic tundra and become a hermit among the polar bears. Nor do we gain a reputation for being the most hateful and difficult neighbor on the block. We learn how to protect our hearts and strive to learn how not to hurt others. We are the walking wounded.

Jesus said, "Come to me, all you who are weary and

burdened, and I will give you rest." (Matt 11:28). Weary from what? Burdened by what? I don't think He was talking about a cement worker or ditch digger who works a hard physical labor job all day. Rather, He has mastered the human plight. He understands the pain of broken relationships, sorrow, guilt, and anger. He is aware the burden we carry when we have not lived up to our own standards, regardless of the expectations of others. He knows when we tire of trying to get ahead in life, trying to find happiness when it eludes us at every turn. He is talking to you and me, the walking wounded.

His rest is the peace and comfort that comes from mercy. He welcomes us into His presence. We are accepted, not condemned. We are loved, not ridiculed. We don't have to jump through any hoops. We can be ourselves, just as we really are. The walking wounded can be healed. The ugliness of our past can melt away.

WRESTLING QUESTIONS

The Walking Wounded

1. How have you been wounded by others in your life?

2. In what ways have you learned to protect yourself?

3. Have you experienced healing from past wounds? How did that happen?

4. Have you hurt other people in your life?

5. How have you promoted healing in those you have hurt?

BIBLICAL TRUTH

The beginning and the end, the Alpha and the Omega, and a lot of stuff in between. As a new believer in my early twenties, I endeavored to read the Bible cover to cover. Before getting to the end of Genesis, I found myself lost in a quagmire of disjointed information, or at least that is how it seemed.

Starting with the creation story, some things just did not make sense. The story starts out with God making different things on subsequent days. While not a Darwinist, I've had enough science in my life to believe that the Earth was formed over a very long period of time. Current scientific consensus is 4.5 billion years, give or take 500 million. Could the presentation have used the word "day" symbolically? Psalm 90:4 tells us that one thousand years is but a day to God. Likewise, a statement made to prove a point and not to be taken literally. How can the God who created the universe be restricted to defining his day based on the revolution of planet Earth in a twenty-four-hour period? God is much bigger than that, and much bigger than we can comprehend.

Also, if Adam and Eve were the first people, who had sons, who did their sons marry? Did Adam and Eve have daughters and the sons then married their sisters? In every culture on Earth, that is a big no-no and can lead to all kinds of genetic problems.

So, what then? Is it possible that there were other people on the Earth? People that God also created? Perhaps Adam and Eve were just the first people that God created with a soul? That doesn't quite make sense either. I don't pretend to know the answer to these questions; I am merely wrestling. When others present as though they have a lock on understanding creation, I question and doubt. Regardless of the details, my search for truth tells me that the universe had a prime mover, and that creator was God.

Perhaps the answer lies with paper. God's chosen people, the Hebrews, were originally flock herders who moved their livestock from pasture to pasture. They lived in tents and moved their entire clan regularly, searching for better pastures, a necessity for a people dependent on their animals for sustenance. Imagine a young child sitting with his parents around the campfire at night, asking a thousand questions: where did the stars come from? Why is the sun so bright and warm and the moon so cold? Why do we have life? How did it start? Why are we here? The answers to these questions might have been developed over many generations, passed on to the next generation by word of mouth.

Does that make the creation story no more than a fairy tale? Absolutely not. As authors of biblical canon penned scripture, God himself surely inspired the tribal oral tradition, too. If one follows the creation story, striking similarities can be seen with scientific findings and assumptions. Could an illiterate sheep herder have fabricated a creation story that so closely matches science? I doubt it. The primary difference is that the biblical presentation refers to things being created in a day as opposed to the scientific data that suggests billions of years.

Besides paper, it is important to note that eastern thought differs from western thought. Eastern thought is focused on the whole concept, not the details. Western thought is analytical, focusing on detail and searching for the who, what, where, when, how, and why. The scientific method is western thought. The broad sweep of creation is eastern thought. Picture a caravan going across the Sahara Desert. Eastern thought would address the destination and the purpose of the trip. Western thought would analyze how many camels, what were they carrying, how many people, and who were they intending to sell or give their products to once they arrived at their destination.

Meanwhile, back to paper. A Bible student will become aware that far greater detail begins to be recorded in the story of Abram in Genesis Chapter 12. Why? The answer is the invention of and the access to paper. Scrolls if you will. Stories could now be recorded and passed on to the next generation without having to rely on memorized stories passed on from one generation to the next.

Must we conclude that the first eleven chapters of Genesis are just a result of someone's imagination? Certainly not. They have rich symbolic meaning. They are stories inspired by God, for the purpose of teaching us about him, so that we may develop a relationship with him. Should we take the creation story literally or symbolically? Should we conclude that these stories are God inspired? A good friend of mine, Barry Franks, once said, "Things that are not heaven and hell issues should not divide us. Salvation is what matters most. I am willing to discuss all parts of the bible, but not interested in creating division on non-salvation topics."

The 39 books of the Old Testament and the 27 books of the New Testament were assembled as canon, regarded as the inspired word of God, a guide for living life and a glimpse into the nature of God. The complete listing of 66 books was first provided by father Athanasius in 367 AD, and gradually accepted by the churches and councils as God inspired.

Some of these writings contain a mistake or two. For example, 2 Kings 23:29-30 states that Judah's King Josiah was killed by Pharaoh's archers in battle at Megiddo, his body then taken back to Jerusalem where he was buried. 2 Chronicles 35:20-24 states that King Josiah was mortally wounded by Pharaoh's archers, and then taken back to Jerusalem, where he died. So, where did he die? Was it on the battlefield or later in Jerusalem? One of them is wrong. Granted, there is an argument for the correct facts being lost in translation from the original manuscripts. But that being the case, we then have even less confidence in the total accuracy of biblical text.

Why point this out? Should we cast doubt on the authenticity of God's word? Should we then throw out the baby with the bath water? No. It is important to read scripture in search of truth. In doing so, we can gain insight into God's story without falling into the trap of worshiping the documents themselves. Scripture has been accepted as God inspired, but remember that it was written by various authors, sometimes multiple authors in the same book, then translated into different languages. Here is the point: Worship God, not the Bible!

A lot of energy is devoted to the study of the end times, the apocalypse, the troubles that will come and then the triumphant return of Jesus. Many followers of the Way have found the Book of Revelation troubling and confusing. Me, too. The book was a vision of John, written at a time of Christian persecution during the reign of the Roman Empire. Many believe that it was a message of hope, written in code, for the church of that day. Contrary to that opinion, many see it as the roadmap of what is yet to come. Even Jesus spoke of the end times. When asked when these things would happen, he said, "But about that day or hour, no one knows, not even the angels in heaven, nor the Son, but only the Father. (Matthew 24:36). He did say that these things would come to pass "before this generation passes away" (Matthew 24:34). Scary thought. Has it already happened? Did we miss it?

I choose not to dwell on the end times. It seems like every generation concludes that it is upon us now. Maybe it is, and if so, great. Meanwhile, my concern is that focusing on something that we cannot know creates a lot of entertainment, but little productivity. We can lose our focus on the importance of doing those things that Jesus told us to do now. I would guess that Satan delights when we chase down a rabbit trail. Jesus also said, "Therefore do not worry about tomorrow, for tomorrow will worry about itself. Each day has enough trouble of its own."

WRESTLING QUESTIONS

Biblical Truth

1. What do you believe about creation?

2. Who did the sons of Adam and Eve marry?

3. What do you believe about Noah, the ark, and the great flood?

4. The bible has literal statements, symbolism, poetry, history, and stories designed to make a point. Jesus used such stories in his parables. How does one sort out the way to understand it?

5. What is your understanding of the end times?

6. Do the end times scare you or are you excited about that time? Is it yet to come?

7. How do you discuss things with others who see the Bible differently than you?

SALVATION

"Are you saved?" the young man asked my sister as she exited the pier in Redondo Beach.

"Yes," she replied.

"Are you really?" he added.

"Yes! Are you?" Her tolerance had turned to irritation.

What happened in this brief exchange? The young man was actively doing what he felt called to do: "Go forth and make disciples." (Matthew 28:19-20). He wanted to spread the good news to strangers, that they might come to a relationship with Jesus, one that he had found and cherished. He may have had a script for saying the "right" salvation words that bring a person to Jesus. So, why did his good intentions turn sour?

The problem might have been in his methodology. My sister perceived his approach as intrusive and judgmental. Most of us have a level of guardedness when out in public. We know that there are people out there who will exploit others, take advantage of them, or even wantonly do bodily harm. They are at least going to try to sell us something.

We also protect our privacy. Few of us will share our personal life with a stranger. Our beliefs about God, and our struggles with our beliefs, are at the core of our very being. The details of our life experience, with all of its joy and pain, are nobody else's business.

Further, we protect ourselves from the judgment of others. Many of us avoid conflict and challenging discussions at all cost because we fear the discomfort of disagreement, the criticism that may be directed at us, and the feeling that, somehow, we are not good enough. Judgment sometimes comes from someone who does not know us, or someone who we do not recognize as having the authority to judge. When this happens, our response is often angry and defensive. We might be tempted to say, "Take that bag of whatever it is you are selling, and go somewhere else. Leave me alone, you Jesus freak!"

So, what was missing? How did the good intentions of that young man become the opposite of his heart's desire?

In his book, *Mere Christianity*, C.S. Lewis spoke of how he was drawn to some of his colleagues at Oxford University. They had something special that he was not readily able to identify. As he got to know them, he discovered that they were Christians. Nothing was "sold" to him. He was not pressured to buy into someone else's beliefs or practices. He just began to want what they had. He wanted that thing that fills that big hole in one's life.

We all have that hole in our lives. God created us that way so that we might discover that He is the only one who can fill it. No amount of worldly things or experiences can fill it beyond, perhaps, a momentary satisfaction. But, long term, those worldly things leave us empty. God fills the hole as we grow in our relationship with Him. In fact, He, the creator of the universe, desires to be in relationship with us, His creation. I confess that I often have a difficult time fully accepting this, though I absolutely believe it. God, the creator of the universe, knows who I am and wants to be in relationship with me! And, you!

"What must I do to inherit eternal life?" asked the rich young ruler. "Go, sell all you have, give to the poor, and follow me," answered Jesus. (Matthew 19:16-22).

Where was the script in that story? Where were the magical words that make us born again? Jesus called the young man to action, to an internal change. He could see that his wealth was the road block to his ability to deepen his relationship with God. The young man was trying to fill the empty place inside him with all the wrong stuff, even though he had been obedient to the commandments and was a good guy.

We can only speculate the long-term outcome for the rich young ruler we just discussed. All we know is that he went away sad, because he had great wealth. Perhaps he wrestled with the importance of keeping his wealth and wanting to follow Jesus. Perhaps he gave up his spiritual pursuit, settling for a life of materialism. Perhaps he had an awakening and followed Jesus' advice.

How about the rest of us? What must we do to gain salvation?

There is a plethora of beliefs. Go down to the alter during a church service altar call, confess your sins, and accept Jesus as your Lord and Savior. What if I did that, but not in a church? Say this script of words and then you will be saved. What if I did that, but did not feel anything? What if I did not say it right? Be baptized, then you are saved. What if I was only sprinkled, not submerged? What if I believe I did it right, but have gone on to continue in all the sins I was doing before? Do I lose my salvation? Some say, "once saved, always saved." Others believe one can fall from grace. What if I never did any of the above, but led a good life? Some say lots of good people are condemned to hell.

Jesus always cut to the heart of the matter, "Who do you say I am?" (Luke 9:20). He had the perfect ability to see a person's heart, what's on the inside. He has the perfect ability to see you and know your heart. Scary, huh? When I first realized that nothing is hidden from Jesus, my emotional reaction was fear. I was afraid of his judgment. I had thoughts that I hid, thoughts that were not good or wholesome. I had done some things in the past that I was not proud of. I condemned myself. How could Jesus not condemn me as well?

Notice how Jesus loved people, even the rich young ruler? Though he turned away in sorrow because of his great wealth, Jesus loved him. For the rest of us, even though we wrestle with the struggles and temptations of this world, Jesus loves us. He loves us beyond our ability to understand it. It is His love, His amazing and unconditional love, that we seek. Nothing else in this world can fill that longing in our hearts. We see evidence of normal people we know trying to fill that void with toys, wealth, sex, drugs, power, prestige, achievements, or something else. Once we come to the place where we realize that none of these things bring us our desired results, the thought of entering a relationship with Jesus becomes possible. We can become open to the idea of a new king in our lives.

We receive salvation by entering into a personal relationship with Jesus. First, I realize that any efforts I make on my own will not fill that spiritual hole inside me. I then can come to the place where I believe that Jesus is the answer, that He and only He can occupy that empty place in my soul. This is what I want, what I have been searching for. Next, I surrender my will to His will. I want Him to guide my feet along the path of life. This salvation is not just an insurance policy, a ticket to eternal life. It is the gateway to a more fulfilling and abundant life now, even as we wrestle with whatever problems today brings. God sees the heart, knowing all our thoughts and actions in total detail. In the middle of all our imperfections, He draws us to Himself and loves us.

To feel the confidence and security of His unfailing love and grace allows me to face life with a positive assurance that, ultimately, God wins. And, I also win.

The term "eat crow" is an idiom referring to the humiliation caused by admitting or having been proven wrong. The crow is a carrion-eater and generates the thought that one must eat something repulsive and emotionally difficult to swallow. However, when "crow" is used as an acronym, the result can be far better: Confess, Repent, Obey, and Worship. Sounds better. This is surrender to a new king, a new lord in my life. Eating crow is not so bad.

Jesus' last commandment was to go forth and make disciples of all nations. (Matthew 28: 19-20). His followers are called to evangelize all people in all nations. Can we accomplish this by standing at the street corner proclaiming that the end is near, repent and be saved? Maybe, but I suspect the success rate will be quite low. Most people will just see some nut yelling on the corner and speculate whether he is homeless or on drugs, or both. So, what then?

Let's go back to C.S. Lewis, who shared that he started out as an atheist. While spending time with colleagues at Oxford, he began to notice that some of them had some quality that he liked. He was drawn to them. He discovered that they were Christians. No one preached to him overtly. But, perhaps, they spread the gospel by sharing who they were, their inner peace and contentment in the face of anything life had to offer. He wanted what they had.

Our challenge as Christians is to take the message to the world by example. As our love for Jesus wells up to overflowing, it will pour out on those around us. Those who are seeking to fill that empty space may see that we have something that they want. This opens the door to sharing the gospel. We can share what Jesus has done in our lives, how being in relationship with him has changed us. We must be "the real deal" without pretense. This requires us to be firmly anchored in our faith, firmly anchored in our relationship with Jesus. We must be honest.

Hebrews 11:1 states that faith is believing in what we have not seen. After Jesus' resurrection, he appeared to the disciples. Thomas, one of the disciples, was not there at the time. When told about Jesus' appearance, Thomas said he would not believe it unless he touched the hole in his side and the hole in his hands. Later, Jesus appeared again while Thomas was there, and told him to touch his piercings. Thomas responded, "My Lord and my God!" (John 20:28). Jesus replied, "Blessed are those who have not seen and yet believe." None of us have seen Jesus, but we have faith that, someday, we will.

Salvation does not come to us by anything we do, apart from saying "yes". In saying "yes" we state that we believe that Jesus is real and that He is who he claimed to be. We are saved by grace through faith. "For it is by grace you have been saved, through faith – and this not from yourselves, it is the gift of God – not by works, so that no one can boast." (Ephesians 2:8-9). We do nothing to deserve it or earn it. John 3:16 tells us that "God so loved the world that he gave his only son, that who so ever believes in him shall not perish, but have everlasting life." This gift is for everyone, without exception, regardless of your tainted past or position in society. "Who so ever" includes you.

WRESTLING QUESTIONS

Salvation

1. Do you consider yourself "saved"?

2. Some people can remember a moment in time, an event, during which they were saved. Many people, especially those who grew up in a church community, just grew up believing and do not have a specific moment of salvation. Does that matter?

3. Must a person say a script of words to anchor or solidify their salvation?

4. What happens to the person who grew up in a country where Christianity was either not preached or was forbidden by the government? Is that person condemned to hell? If Jesus is the only way, what happens to the millions of people like that person?

5. We often concern ourselves over the salvation of a friend or relative. Can we leave it in God's hands and put our trust in His plan, His ways?

6. Acknowledging that salvation is in God's hands, do we still play a part? Jesus called us to go forth and make disciples (Matthew 28:19-20). How do we do that?

PRAYER

Have you ever been frustrated with your prayer life? I certainly have. There have been times when I questioned whether God was even listening. Scripture says that He hears every prayer and He knows what you want even before you ask (Psalm 139:1-4). But, often, it does not feel like He is listening.

I recall a debate in a Bible study class years ago where a fellow classmate declared that he did not believe in modern day miracles, that God basically set things up and now is on vacation. The question came up as to whether God remains actively involved in His creation. Since people pray to God when they or loved ones are in trouble, often asking for a miracle, the issue of prayer came up. Asking God to bend the normal physics of our world, asking for a miracle, is futile if He is not listening. So, why bother with prayer? Most of us believe that God does listen and, further, that He is omnipresent. He is everywhere all at once, or at least He can be if He chooses to do so.

Even when we believe God is actively involved, those of us who have experienced the silence of God to our prayers can get the feeling that we are not doing it right. Why else would I get the impression that I am talking to no one? To make things worse, we know devout Christians that believe God hears all their petitions and gives them answers constantly, even to petty and trivial things. "God told me which brand of deodorant to buy." Really? I doubt that He cares. I doubt that He wants to have input into whether I pick blue jeans or black jeans for the day. I have always felt that He gave me abilities to make those and many other choices, and that I am expected to use those abilities as much as I can.

However, there is a risk. The better I get at solving problems and getting the job done, the less I recognize my need for Him. Perhaps I will become too independent and arrogant. I do believe in the "still, small voice" of the Holy Spirit in my head, nudging me along the way towards the ultimate goal. Has a person ever just popped into your mind and you felt the desire to call that person? Later, you learned that person was in crisis and really could have used your support and friendship. Spiritual nudges can come along in big things like marriage and career decisions. They can also come along in small ways like deciding to turn left instead of right, only to find out later that there was a major traffic accident you might have been involved in if you had gone with your first impulse. The mystery is that somebody did turn that way and was involved in the accident. Why? I have no idea. Another mystery with which I must wrestle.

Maybe the "dry spell" in my prayer life is my own fault. It is hard to focus when I have the attention span of a kindergartner. My mind wanders and sometimes I even fall asleep. Sorry, Lord. At times, I am guilty of just conducting a one-way conversation, asking for all the things I think are right and needed, but not acknowledging His sovereignty, His omnipotence (all powerful), and His omniscience (all knowing). I also fail to listen.

Once in my life, I heard an audible answer to my prayer. I was under great stress and could not sleep, deeply troubled by the social and cultural divisions in a company that I was supposed to be leading. I crawled out of bed and got on my knees, "Lord, please help me with this situation. I have tried everything I know how to do and nothing is working. In fact, things keep getting worse! Please tell me what to do and I will do it." The response was loud and clear, "You are doing it!" My head jerked up, expecting to see someone in the room standing before me. I saw no one. For a moment, I was shocked into silence.

"Doing what? I am not doing anything!" I declared as I returned to prayer. I needed more detail, more clarification, more guidance. Or, so I thought. No further answer was forthcoming. I was left not really knowing or understanding what it was that I was doing. But I did have a comfort that I must be doing something right.

I have never received an audible response to prayer since, and that was nearly thirty years ago. Some people claim that God speaks to them all the time. I confess that I often suspect that they are possibly fooling themselves. They want to have that special and personal communication so strongly that they convince themselves that their own mental processing is God literally speaking to them. Their desire overrides reality. They may be seeking the experience so badly because their fellow Christians are doing it, and they want to fit in. After all, I am just as good of a Christian as they are!

Obviously, I wrestle with the validity of their assertions. Maybe they have what they claim. Maybe I am the one with the problem. Perhaps He is speaking all the time and some of us are just not very good at listening. Do I neglect, ignore, or even resist that still, small voice that speaks to me? At times, His silence may indicate that He trusts me to make a good decision. Sometimes, I may be hearing His voice and mistakenly attributing it to my own thoughts. Therefore, I must be vigilant in discerning and testing that which I hear.

Jesus said, "And when you pray, do not be like the hypocrites, for they love to pray standing at the synagogues and on the street corners to be seen by men. I tell you the truth, they have received their reward in full. But when you pray, go into your room, close the door and pray to your Father, who is unseen. Then your Father, who sees what is done in secret, will reward you. And when you pray, do not keep on babbling like pagans, for they think they will be heard because of their many words. Do not be like them, for your Father knows what you need before you ask him. This, then, is how you should pray:

> "Our Father in heaven, hallowed be your
>   name.
> Your kingdom come, your will be done
>   on earth as it is in heaven.
> Give us today our daily bread.
> Forgive us our debts, as we forgive our
>   debtors.
> And lead us not into temptation, but
>   deliver us from the evil one."
> For if you forgive men when they sin
>   against you, your heavenly Father will
>   also forgive you. But, if you do not
>   forgive men their sins, your Father
>   will not forgive your sins.

— MATTHEW 6:5-15

This wonderful and perfect prayer makes us feel good. But, notice that it is followed with a pinch of accountability.

Prayer is all about our relationship with God. When we confess our own selfishness or misdeeds, we are confessing to God what he already knows. When we ask for His attention to some aspect in our lives or the lives of others, He already sees what is on our hearts. He already understands what we think about Him, even when we are mad or disappointed by His non-compliance with what we "know" to be best. He also perceives when we are humble enough to be thankful for the blessings we have already received and continue to receive.

So, why pray? He already knows everything. If God were only a cosmic butler, there to provide us with the services we ask for, prayer would be as shallow as a vending machine. But prayer is about our relationship with Him, prayer becomes critical for us to grow closer to Him, to understand within our own hearts that He knows us, to feel His support, and to listen to Him.

Listening is the hardest part for many of us. I have heard leaders of group prayer that are so elegant, their words flowing beautifully and full of meaning. Those leaders spoke their hearts so wonderfully. I wish I could speak prayer like that. But there is a second ingredient to prayer that may be missing; the art of listening. We need to really listen for that "still small voice" that speaks to our hearts. To me, this is something akin to meditation, clearing my mind of all my own stuff and paying attention to that voice that may or may not come. I refer to this as an art because it can be difficult to achieve. I must learn to wait upon the Lord. (Isa 40:31). Distractions, boredom, impatience, and a short attention span constantly get in the way. I confess my need to develop this art form of listening in prayer.

For those of us that are spiritually or intellectually challenged, there are prayer methods that can help. There are many, so I will only mention one: The acronym is ACTS: Adoration, Confession, Thanksgiving, and Supplication. Start your prayer with adoration, the expression of love for His love, kingship, sovereignty, majesty, and glory. Then confess those things you need to confess, whether in the recent or distant past. Thirdly, express thanksgiving for the blessings you have received in your life. These are easy to find, even in tough times. Lastly, ask Him for those things that are on your mind, things where you would like to see His intervention. Ask that they be in accordance with His will and not just your own will. One thing must be added to ACTS; Listen. We must work on clearing our minds and developing the art of listening.

WRESTLING QUESTIONS

Prayer

1. Do you believe God hears your prayers?

2. How often do your pray?

3. Do you have set times when you pray or do you pray randomly during the day?

4. Do you believe that God answers your prayers? How?

5. Do your prayers need to be eloquently spoken, or can it be your words, your way?

6. Are you happy with your prayer life?

7. How can you improve your prayer life?

8. Why is prayer even important?

DOUBT

Have you ever had doubts about whether all this God stuff is real? Is there really a God? Did a virgin actually conceive a child from God? Seems impossible. If we accept that much, did Jesus, the son of God, really die for our sins, especially considering that we were not to be born for another two thousand years? Is grace really freely given? Real life experience teaches us that nothing is free.

Some of us have doubt questions most of the time, some of us seldom. Almost everyone has had doubts at different times in their lives. Those doubts can be during times of loss or crisis. How could a loving God let this happen? Or they can come when there does not seem to be anything much happening in our lives at all. Perhaps doubt can creep in during a dry spell in our prayer life.

In many churches, it is not OK to have doubt. We are perceived as weak or a person of little faith. We are lumped in with Thomas, the "show me" disciple that said he would not believe that Jesus had risen until he had seen the holes in his hands and the pierce in his side (John 20:25). Like Thomas, we want some tangible proof.

As a young philosophically searching college student, very open minded, I questioned that anyone could know absolute truth. My brother, six years older, said he had found The Truth. Upon my challenge, he merely stated that I was not ready for it yet. He was right. I could not accept The Truth until I came to the point of accepting it as a matter of faith (Hebrews 11:1). Upon doing that, the Holy Spirit assured me that, indeed, The Truth was found in God and that The Truth will continue to be revealed to me through the Holy Spirit (John 14:15-31).

Though I am convinced that there is an absolute truth, none of us can fully know or grasp that truth. That is God's business. We are merely his children, made in his image, dwelling in earthly bodies, on a life-long quest to become closer to the truth. Our business is to continually seek the truth. Jesus said, "I am the way and the truth and the life. No one comes to the Father except through me." (John 14:6). The danger for us is the temptation to believe that we have arrived, that we know how it all works, that we have the answers. We need to humble ourselves or risk the temptation of becoming like the Pharisees; judgmental, arrogant, condescending, and prideful.

What if our doubts are closer to reality? What if religion really is just an opiate for the masses? What if we really did evolve from pond scum? In that case, nothing really matters. Values do not mean anything. Love does not count for much other than a silly emotion. Family bonds are insignificant. Society's values and personal values are meaningless. Then, there really is no purpose to existence. There is no right or wrong. Depressing, huh? Whether we are believers or not, we know deep down that there must be something more.

Even an atheist has the need for something more. A person who does not believe that God exists still has strong feelings about right and wrong. There is still a passion for justice in society, orderly co-existence, and a sense of fairness. Even the non-believer wants to protect others from discrimination, abuse, and exploitation. She wants to be kind, loving, and helpful. He has a need to see himself as a "good" person. He might even go so far as to sacrifice his life in order to save a stranger from harm, taking a bullet to save the innocent. But, wait! That behavior is counter-intuitive to our survival instincts. That type of person should gradually become eliminated from the gene pool. But they are not. Even non-believers are drawn to that which is good, that which is found in the image of God.

To have doubt is normal. In fact, it is a necessary ingredient to personal growth. When I have doubts, I need to find the answers. When I have doubts about whether or not it will rain, I need to research the weather channels. If I doubt whether we will arrive on time, I can calculate my ETA (estimated time of arrival). When I have doubts about my faith, I can go to the Bible and search related scriptures, ask a fellow Christian who I believe has deeper knowledge than I, pray with an open heart, and apply my own reasoning abilities. Though doubt may never fully go away, we get better at wrestling with this issue as we mature in our faith.

WRESTLING QUESTIONS

Doubt

1. Have you ever had doubts about all of this "God stuff"?

2. If you came to the decision that God does not exist, do you ever question that decision?

3. Have you ever doubted whether Jesus is who He claimed to be?

4. If you have been a Christian for some time, does doubt occasionally still creep in?

5. Is it really OK to have doubts, or is that a sign of weakness?

6. Do doubts make you a bad person?

7. Can we grow from working through our periods of doubt?

8. Are doubts and unbelief the same thing?

SIN

Sin consists of those thoughts and actions that separate us from God.

You may have heard "Sin is sin," meaning that all sins are equal. They are equal in that all sins drive a wedge between us and God. In this worldly life and our physical bodies, we often choose our own wants and desires at the expense of breaking God's laws and creating that separation.

Acknowledging that, I have a difficult time accepting that all sins are equal. It is impossible for me to treat the murder of six million Jewish people orchestrated by Adolph Hitler during World War II the same as a neighbor who cheats on his taxes. Or, the horror of war in the invasion of Ukraine caused by the crazed ambitions of a monster, Putin, compared to someone who accepted change from the cashier for a twenty when he only gave her a ten-dollar bill. Even Jesus referred to the concept of "greater" sin when He said,

"Woe to the one who causes one of these little ones to sin..." (Matthew 18:6). It seems that the greater sins are the ones that have greater consequences on others. Mankind's inhumanity to mankind is often the definition of evil.

You may also have heard of the seven deadly sins; pride, greed, wrath, envy, lust, gluttony, and sloth. Though originally developed in the early Egyptian Christian school of Alexandria, Pope Gregory refined the list in 500 AD. This list is not found anywhere in the Bible, but each sin is addressed in many places throughout the Old and New Testaments. These are the foundational sins that lead to other sins. For example, lust leads to adultery, greed leads to stealing, and envy leads to jealousy. So, are these seven more deadly than other sins? It seems like all sins lead to death if there is no way out through grace and forgiveness.

If sin is sin, as many who are solidly anchored in their faith will say, then why do we make such a big deal out of some sins and minimize or ignore others? We tend to write off the hostile and degrading comments fellow Christians make about the "other" political party. We rationalize that they are just passionate about our country. This somehow justifies their bad and un-Christ-like behavior. Another good Christian has a habit of embellishing stories; that big one that got away because a thirty-point buck being chased by a mountain lion splashed through the creek just as he was setting the hook. Again, we let the sin pass as we assess that the fisherman must have a poor self-image and needs people to like him.

After all, he really is not hurting anyone. Right? Or, is he?

Ah, but when it comes to sexual sin, everyone gets interested! Mom found a pornographic magazine under her teenage son's mattress. She panics. She may later discover that her son stole the magazine from his dad. Adulterers destroying their marriages, reaping havoc on the children, disgracing their parents and church community. Counseling and true repentance may salvage the situation. A homosexual comes out of the closet. Oh, no! The ultimate abomination! Forget counseling. He or she is going to burn in hell. Ouch! Do we act like "sin is sin"? We quickly went from grace and forgiveness to judgment and condemnation. I pray that God is not as harsh as we tend to be. God seeks relationship, not destruction.

Perhaps the reasons we get so excited about sexual sin is that we closely identify with it. My judgmental reaction is based on either fear or guilt. Upon hearing of infidelity and adultery, my emotional reaction is harsh judgment. How could that person be so disloyal? How could they so badly hurt the people they love the most? Yet, inside my private thoughts I know that I am no better, even when I have not acted on it. Jesus said, "But I tell you that anyone who looks at a woman lustfully has already committed adultery with her in his heart." (Matthew 5:28). So, try as I might to "be good," I fail. I am sunk. Everyone is sunk. You are sunk. What man or woman can say that they have never looked at another person lustfully? So, we bear the burden of our own thoughts. We fear that we will be exposed. We feel guilty that we are so impure. Guilt and fear. The only way most of us feel better is to say that we are not as bad as the other guy or gal. Too late. God already knows all your inner thoughts and, lucky you, He loves you in spite of yourself. Our only hope is forgiveness and grace. We must learn to be honest with ourselves and with God, since He knows anyway, and seek relationship with the true source of goodness.

It is all about relationships. We do not exist in a void. We each have a relationship with ourself, commonly referred to as our self-image. Whether or not we like ourselves often determines how we treat ourselves. Most of us have seen someone who seemed bent on self-destruction, stemming from fulfilling what they thought they deserved. Someone with a positive self-image often seems more content and able to have positive relationships with others. Some drive themselves to be successful financially to battle the feelings that, deep down, they know that they really do not like what they see.

We have relationships with other people. We are someone's child, spouse, sibling, parent, grandparent, coworker, boss, subordinate, friend, classmate, or nearby stranger in public. None of us would have survived infancy without someone taking care of us. Someone fed and protected us from harm. Someone nurtured and loved us while we were too little to understand or even to love them back. All of us had parents, good or bad. None of us had perfect parents. The impact of parents on their children's lives cannot be overstated. Blessed is the person who had good parenting, for that person will be better able to pass on that blessing to their own children. Those children can thrive.

Our relationship with God is critical in that ability to thrive, to become all that we were meant to be. He desires for us to have the abundant life. Jesus said, "I came that you might have life, and have it to the full." (John 10:10). In relationship with Him, that fullness of life is possible, regardless of our current life circumstances and regardless of our past. He was talking about that place inside each of us that only He can fill. As mentioned, none of us had perfect earthly parents. In Him, we have the perfect heavenly parent, who loves us beyond our ability to understand and wants to draw us close to Him. In Him, there is love, joy, peace, and healing. Everything that is wrong in me can be taken away. I can thrive. I can be forgiven of all the mistakes, mishaps, and sins of my past.

When my father went into the hospital for the last time, he knew he was dying. Having seen my growing faith, he asked me, "What must I do to be saved?" I responded with the common response, "Confess your sins, surrender to Him, and ask Him to be the lord and master of your life."

"I've done that, but I still don't feel it!" he exclaimed. Dad still had doubts. He still had the feeling that he was not good enough. He still struggled with harsh judgment of himself.

"Jesus has forgiven you. The only thing you have left to do is to forgive yourself," I replied. Dad found no peace in my answer. To this day, I feel that my response was the right thing to say. I remain unsure of whether my statement was from my psychology background or spirit led. Since I am now sharing it with you, I vote for the later. We cannot forgive our own sins, only the one we have sinned against can forgive us. If we sin against God, only he can forgive us. If we sin against another person, only that person can forgive us. If we sin against ourselves, harming our own self-image, the problem persists when we continue to beat ourselves up after we have been forgiven. It is easy to destroy yourself in self-condemnation.

I imagine that Dad is now in Heaven. When he met Jesus, I can imagine Jesus saying, "Dave, your son was right. I have forgiven you. Quit beating yourself up. Welcome to my family. We shall enjoy love and fellowship for eternity."

So, if it is all about relationships, sin consists of those thoughts and actions that drive a wedge into those relationships. When Jesus said he came that we might have life to the full, He was talking about living in harmony with God, with others, and even within ourselves. Sin melts away when I put God before self and when I put others before self. Surprisingly, I become much happier and content when I can get beyond myself. That can be difficult to do since I am contained in this mind and body. People who are self-focused are often the most miserable folks in the neighborhood. When I strive to heal rather than hurt, to lift up rather than tear down, my life gets better and so do the lives of those around me.

WRESTLING QUESTIONS

Sin

1. Do you believe that "sin is sin"?

2. Why is sexual sin seen as worse than other sins?

3. Why is homosexuality deemed to be worse than heterosexual adultery and fornication?

4. Is there a relationship between the sin and the gravity of the consequences?

5. Do you see your behavior as sinful if nobody else is getting hurt?

6. Are you a better Christian than the person next to you if your sins are less in comparison?

JUDGEMENT

Do not judge, or you too will be judged.

— MATTHEW 7:1

Take a brother and go and confront that person.

— MATTHEW 18:15-17

Woe to you teachers of the law and pharisees, you hypocrites! You give a tenth of your spices-mint, dill, and cumin. But you have neglected the more important matters of the law-justice, mercy, and faithfulness. You should have practiced the latter, without neglecting the former. You blind guides! You strain out a gnat but swallow a camel.

— MATTHEW 23:23-24

Confusing, isn't it? We are called not to judge and we are called to correct one another. The challenge is to help guide each other along the path of spiritual growth. The problem often lies in not fully understanding the circumstances and prematurely rushing to judgment. I must confess, one of the things I love to do is judge harshly those who judge harshly.

The Pharisees were the religious leaders of Jesus' day. They were considered knowledgeable holy men who had their act together. They were respected in the community, given the best seats in the synagogue, and instructed the people on what they must do in order to be in a right relationship with God. The modern equivalent would be a rabbi, priest, or pastor.

Today, those of us who consider ourselves Christians and have been at it for a while, run the risk of placing ourselves in the seat of judgement. Like the Pharisees, we have studied God's law, we have been forgiven, we know what others should be doing. And, sometimes, we think we know whether their efforts in developing a relationship with God are being done right. The danger is to become self-righteous, condescending, and arrogant.

Have I the right to be self-righteous? Am I now "pure"? Jesus said, "Take the log out of your own eye before you attempt to take the speck out of someone else's eye." (Matthew 7:5). Have I the right to be condescending? Am I better than anyone else? Am I better than the homeless guy living under a bridge? With my growing confidence in my knowledge and my growing assurance that I am one of the chosen ones, should arrogance permeate my relationships? Jesus came to minister to exactly those people who literally or symbolically are "living under the bridge". He came for everyone, in fact, not just us good guys. Am I in a position to judge others? If I can muster even one once of humility, certainly I will conclude that I am not.

Yet, that is exactly what we do. We judge people's work performance, their misguided politics, their misguided parenting practices, their pitiful efforts at following their religious beliefs, and even their clothes and haircut. Some time ago, I heard a statement that in effect said, "When the rapture comes, everyone in that house will still be there. There is no Holy Spirit in that house." Done deal. Judgement has been passed. Period.

My mother married my father, who had been married before. Her sister-in-law once told her, "Louise, you know you are going to hell," because of this "sin" of marrying someone who had already once been married. Once again, done deal. In the woman's mind, my mother was choosing to continue to live in sin. Condemned. Judgment has been passed. Mom's reaction was, "Well, if that is the case, why bother?" Her response was to reject her sister-in-law's belief and quit going to the church that fostered that belief. She saw the hypocrisy and judgmental environment of that church where grace seemed to be missing.

How did we come to position ourselves in the judgment seat? How did we become this discerning? How did we conclude that Mom would burn in hell and whether anyone in that house was to be left out of the rapture? Do we know whether they had once said the magic words of salvation? If they did, then is their salvation lost? How do we know how Jesus looks upon them, even though there is no outward evidence of practicing faith the way we say it should be practiced? Do we know their inner thoughts and whether they ever pray, reaching out to a God that they do not fully understand? Do we fully understand God? Do we have a right to judge? I sense that love and grace are missing in our rush to judgement.

In becoming judgmental, we often weaponize scripture. We cherry pick those scriptures that support our position or argument. Proverbs 13:24 says, "Whoever spares the rod hates their children, but the one who loves their children is careful to discipline them." So, I can self-righteously quote that scripture to unleash my anger on my kids? I can criticize someone else's parenting practices, stating that they are going to ruin their children and just raise a bunch of brats? What if my position backfires on me? What if my children grow up with hurt and anger instead of love and nurturance? Oops!

In addition to weaponizing scripture, we become judgmental in denominationalism. My church is better than your church. Are Mormon's going to burn in hell or are they the one true church? Do Catholics even know who Jesus is? How about those wishy-washy Methodists? Yeah, God is going to spit them out! By the way, even though you were baptized in the Baptist church across town, you need to be re-baptized at our Baptist church because those guys do not have it quite right. Ah, the Devil's playground!

Romans 2:1 says, "You, therefore, have no excuse, you who pass judgement on someone else, for at whatever point you judge another, you are condemning yourself, because you who pass judgement are doing the same things." I encourage you to look it up and read it, but do not stop with just verse one. Read the entire chapter. Wrestle with the issue of judgment.

Sometimes we cannot help but notice when someone is engaging in actions that will be harmful to self or others. We feel compelled to do something about it, to intervene. If we rush in with only partial understanding, we can do more harm than good. We must first seek to understand. Then, we must examine and question our own values and motives. What is the reason that we feel the need to intervene? Is it an emotional reaction within us from our own past experiences? It is not necessarily a bad thing to share those experiences, having stood on the tracks with an oncoming train.

We must seek to judge rightly. Right judgment speaks in truth, truth that is tempered with love. Right judgment is focused on the problem while not condemning the person. We want to build up, not tear down. We strive to restore a person gently, showing the same love and compassion that we see in Jesus. Our own thoughts and motives must be tested and we must seek God's guidance as we attempt to intervene, following His example.

WRESTLING QUESTIONS

Judgement

1. What emotions are kindled in me when you feel judged by others?

2. Do you ever "rush to Judgement"?

3. What is the difference between righteous judgement and unrighteous judgement?

4. How often do you judge others?

5. What is your heart's desire when you judge others? Do you judge out of love or is it sometimes mean spirited?

6. Have you ever weaponized scripture, using it to harshly judge someone?

7. Do you see a difference in the judgment that comes from people and the judgment that comes from God?

BLAME

Flip Wilson, a very successful comedian in the late 1960's and 1970's, won the hearts of millions of Americans with his famous line, "The Devil made me do it!" The look on his face made it obvious that he really did not believe what he was saying. Rather, he was looking for someone else to blame. Whatever we imagined that he did wrong, he clearly was trying to duck out of taking any personal responsibility. He did not want to accept the potential consequences of his own actions; he didn't want to look bad in the eyes of others. His presentation of this common internal battle was very funny.

Looking for someone or something else to blame has been the human plight throughout all recorded history. When God questioned Adam and Eve after they had eaten the forbidden fruit, He knew exactly what they had done. Adam blamed Eve, who then blamed the serpent. Their shallow defense did not get them out of trouble and only further compounded the problem. (Genesis

3:8-13). The consequences proved to be quite severe (Genesis 3:14-19). One may wonder how things would have turned out if both Adam and Eve had just openly confessed their disobedience and taken full responsibility for their own actions.

I have long been an advocate of taking full responsibility for my own thoughts and actions. While I acknowledge that Satan exists, I choose not to blame him for even the most subtle of thoughts that might enter my head. Most of us have heard someone say that the devil is putting temptation before you and he knows how to manipulate your weaknesses. Stay on guard from Satan's attacks! While this may be true, I find little value in watching my back and living in paranoia of the bad guy lurking in the shadows. I would rather follow the example Jesus set when he said, "Away from me, Satan! It is written: 'Worship the Lord your God, and serve him only'." (Matthew 4:10). It seems that the more I dwell on Satan, the more room I give him to wander into my life. The result is living in fear. I much prefer to dwell on Jesus, the giver of life, the giver of love. I have much more trust and confidence in His intent for my life. It is also a lot more fun. Satan has no power in the face of Jesus. Choose your friends wisely.

So, the Devil did not make me do it. I made me do it. I am the one who chose to pursue my original bad thought. I am the one who chose to eventually act on that thought I knew to be wrong. In being truly honest with myself, I can be honest in my relationship with God. He already knows all my thoughts anyway. He is already aware of my weaknesses, excuses, justifications, and denials. When I approach Him just as I am, openly, without pretense, asking his forgiveness and mercy for my shortcomings and imperfections, I trust Him to be a God of mercy, forgiveness, grace, and truth. His love and faithfulness will sustain me and restore me into a right relationship with Him.

This feels like the weight of my misdeeds has been lifted from my shoulders. There is no reason to continue to beat myself up for those missteps. I am free to move forward knowing that I have been made whole. I do not have to make the same bad choices that I have made in the past. I do not have to live in the shadows of guilt. I do have to be honest with myself and with Him.

We followers of the Way should, therefore, live daily lives of joy and happiness. Regardless of our circumstances, we have the amazing love and grace of our Lord in our lives. We have been made whole. We have the best friend anyone could ever want or desire. When Jesus went to the cross, He in effect said, "I am not responsible for your sin, but I will pay the price for you so that you and I can be in a right relationship with each other." Why, then, do so many of us go through our daily lives burdened with the worries of the world? Are we called to be suffering servants who lead lives of misery in order to prove our worthiness to God? Wallowing in my misery as a suffering servant allows me to indulge and nurture myself, to "lick my wounds," but it accomplishes nothing of value. It is better to serve willingly and without the downtrodden demeanor, without the suffering. I choose to serve willingly and joyfully, because of the one who chose me.

Can I accomplish the practice of serving joyfully in a world that is so messed up? The world seems full of evil and danger. Morality is constantly being bashed and challenged. Violent crime is far too common. Justice in our legal system appears to be failing. Political and social issues are tearing society apart. Corruption is everywhere. Fires, floods, and other natural disasters are on the rise. Was this all part of God's master plan? Why is an omnipotent, omniscient, and omnipresent God allowing such horrible things to go on in the world? Why doesn't He intervene? If God has planned all this struggle and mayhem, then is God the one to blame?

Blaming God makes most of us feel like we are on dangerous ground, but that is exactly what we do. We pray that God will heal a friend or family member from a deadly disease. When that person's health is restored, we praise God and give Him the credit for a miracle. When the person dies, we tend to say that it was his or her time and God took our friend home. Either way, it is God's fault. He is to blame. Some of us have even become angry at God for not sparing someone we love. We know that he could have restored their health. I cringe when I hear of a Christian with the best of intentions trying to comfort a grieving parent by saying, "Your child is with God now. God just loved her so much that he wanted to take her home." What a cruel thing to say. The grieving parent loved their child deeply. It is a cruel and selfish

God that would rob me of my child so that He could have her.

The grieving parents may even turn on themselves because it is not OK to blame God. This must be my fault. My child was taken from me because of some known or unknown sin from my past. I blame myself. Beware! Self-condemnation is dangerous ground. It is often rooted in a life experience of being rejected by others or judged harshly. It can result in further misery or even tragedy. In truth, God does not inflict this kind of pain on us. We have a loving God, full of grace, love, mercy, and truth.

Children sometimes have a propensity for accepting the blame for things that were beyond their control. They tend to see their parents as being whole and being the example to follow. They have no other life experience. So, if mom and dad are getting divorced, children often feel that they are somehow to blame. If I got better grades in school, they would stay together. Dad would not beat me if I did a better job on my chores. Mom drinks because I am a bad child. This misguided sense of guilt and blame can carry into adulthood, even after life experience and logic tell us otherwise. It takes a great deal of discernment and clarity, sometimes therapy, to know when to accept personal blame and when to put the blame at the true source.

Sometimes, bad things just happen. A great deal of conflict resides in me when I cannot resolve the thought of God being in control of every little detail and the thought of random occurrences that go along with the laws of nature that God created. So, is it possible that God created the laws of nature but does not micro-manage every little detail? Harold S. Kushner addresses undeserved suffering and blame in his book, *When Bad Things Happen To Good People.*

Rabbi Kushner's book dedicates a whole chapter to Job, one of the books of the Old Testament. Job is a great treatise on suffering, blame, and relationships. The book is believed by many to be more of a fable than historical fact, similar to the way Jesus used parables to teach His messages. As the story goes, God allows Satan to strip Job of all his wealth and blessings, so that Satan's assertion that Job only worships God because of those blessings can be tested. Very quickly, Job's herds are destroyed or stolen, all his children die, and he becomes stricken with painful body sores. His wife tells him to curse God and die. His friends come to console him, only to end up blaming him for some unknown sin that has brought all this calamity upon him. Another observer later adds that God has done these things to Job in order to humble him.

Throughout the ordeal, Job neither blames God or himself. He asserts his innocence. When Job questions God, God answers him out of a storm. (Job 38-41). In detail, God says, in effect, "Who are you to question me? Can you do the things that I have done? Do you present yourself as being equal to me?" Jobs answer shows his humility, claiming himself to be unworthy and putting his hand over his mouth. (Job 40:4-5). At the end of the story, everything that Job lost is restored to him and more.

Yet, the questions of blame, suffering and fairness are never fully resolved. Rabbi Kushner asserts that the God we know to be good and loving must not be all powerful. God will walk alongside us in our suffering, but there are things that He is unable to fix. This position is comforting from the standpoint of not holding God responsible for everything, as in "God, why do you allow this? Why don't you fix this? Why did you allow this to happen in the first place?" If God did not do this to me, then I am off the hook for blaming Him. I can approach Him for comfort, love, and resolution.

However, if He is the God of the universe, the prime mover in the "big bang" who created something out of nothing, then He is all powerful. He is omnipotent. All my worldly problems could be fixed by Him with the snap of his fingers. All the woes of the world are like child's play to Him. Yet, bad things happen to good people, life is seldom fair, and sometimes the bad guy wins.

As I was writing the above two paragraphs on a Sunday evening, our dog ran out in our backyard only to get sprayed by a skunk. I cannot count the number of times I have had to de-skunk him. Why can't my dog learn? Why do I keep him? Why did God make skunks? Why didn't He make my dog smarter? It is not fair. I did not do anything wrong. Yet, I am stuck with the conse- quences of fumes rolling in our open windows and cleaning up the dog. I do not like my dog very much right now, but I know we'll keep him. We love that stupid dog! We are not going to blame God for the putrid method He gave skunks to defend themselves. I am not going to blame my wife for opening the door to let our dog out. Welcome to life. Life happens at the intersection of a dog being a dog and a skunk being a skunk. I do not know why. I just have to accept whatever life brings, skunks and all.

It is far better to say, "I don't know," than to try and provide a theological answer to life's tragedies. Comfort comes through relationships, not theology.

WRESTLING QUESTIONS

Blame

1. Have you ever blamed God for some loss or tragedy in your life?

2. Do you ever use excuses, denial, or rationalizations to avoid accepting responsibility?

3. Have you ever accepted the blame for something that you know logically was beyond your control?

4. Is God in control of every little detail in our lives? If so, what is the consequence of that?

5. Is there any value in assigning blame in every situation?

TRIBE

My son and daughter-in-law had several different types of chickens. Not only were their eggs a little different, they looked different in size, shape, and the pattern of their feathers. Each tended to congregate with their own kind, and often were unkind to the other chickens; birds of a feather, I suppose.

We are not so different from the chickens. We are drawn to churches that think, act, and believe in ways that are compatible with our own views. Many people take the time and effort to study the theological views and positions of a church before they commit to attending worship services. Others attend the services of multiple churches in hopes of finding the shoe that fits, without any preliminary research. Either method can be successful, especially when the church offers orientation or new membership classes.

All of this is fine until the chickens start feeling the need for all of us to be homogenous. The Republican chickens sit in these pews; the Democrats sit over there. Do not sit in those pews; they are frequented by California chickens! More realistically, we start feeling that everyone should have the same view of creation, the correct way of doing baptisms, and when a person should or should not raise their hands in worship, say "Amen," or shout "Praise the Lord." How about speaking in tongues or dancing in the isles? Yes, we all have our comfort or discomfort levels with what to believe, how to think and how to behave in church.

Some denominations demand more homogeny than others. I think all churches demand some level even when they are unaware of it. We want a tribe that we are comfortable with, and anyone who thinks or behaves too far out from our comfort zone creates anxiety and discomfort. This is the primary reason we have so many different denominations within the greater Christian church. Generally, having multiple denomination choices is perfectly fine. People can find the church where they feel connected in the way that church body worships God. Specifically for Christians, the key is that the church is worshiping the correct God; God the Father, Jesus the Son our Savior, and His Holy Spirit.

Pastor Austin Bender once said that the number one thing that drives people away from Christian churches is Christians! Suppose I attend your church for the first time. I am feeling a little uncomfortable because I don't know all of the expectations of this church, the order of worship, when to sit or stand, or even where to sit. I do not know the words to the songs, a dead giveaway that I am a newbie. Will anyone greet me or ask my name? If no one welcomes me, should I just find a place to sit so that I am away from everybody else? What if I am part Californian and I hear some subtle but harsh comments directed at Californians? What if I feel the judgmental stare coming out of the corner of the eye of the "old school" gentleman down the pew from me? I am not dressed the same and I look a lot different.

I came to your church today because of a need in my life to connect with God, at least I think that is why I came. Honestly, I am not even sure why I came and doing so might have been a mistake. I do not feel comfortable. The thought crossed my mind that if these good church people knew the real me, I would be thrown out the door and invited to never come back.

Some of my concern melted away as the church service got underway. The music was uplifting. The sermon was pretty good and there were some moments when I thought the pastor was speaking directly to me. So far, so good.

Afterwards, the pastor encouraged people to head for Fellowship Hall and share some coffee and conversation. Most people congregated in small groups of three or four and, by the looks of their interaction, must already know each other well. My coffee was a little too hot, so I had to sip it slowly as I stood there watching everyone. The need to get out of there started to grow and I wish I had not taken a cup of coffee, which now seemed to be holding me back. After a few long minutes, the cup went in the trash and I was headed for the door.

Exodus interruptus. A little old lady with a pleasant, disarming smile stopped me. I'll bet she is the favorite of her grandchildren. She asked my name, followed by a host of other questions. Her interest seemed sincere and I did not get a sense that she was "interrogating" me. She was nice and seemed genuinely interested in me, although I am not sure why. I asked about her as our conversation continued. Though she freely shared information about her life, she regularly turned the topic of conversation back to me. As we parted ways sometime later, I left the building feeling better. Maybe I will come back next week. I know one person now; Mrs. Johnson.

Why is it so hard for members of the congregation to reach out to new people? Why was Mrs. Johnson the only one who did? There are many reasons. First, when we go to church, we see people that we are connected to and we want to catch up on how their lives are going. This is good, but it runs the risk of monopolizing our limited time. Second, what if the "new" person I approach has been attending there for a long time? Embarrassing! I should have known that. Third, I am terrible at remembering names. This also gets embarrassing. Fourth, perhaps I am not good at meeting new people. I do not like that awkward and forced small talk. Maybe the person I approach will not want to talk to me. Fifth, sometimes I am just in a bad mood or dealing with a bunch of problems of my own. I am too wrapped up in myself to have the energy or time for someone else. Sixth, and most dangerous, perhaps I do not really care if a new person comes back or not. Ouch!

After attending a church for several months, we begin to see that those perfect people really are not so perfect. They are all dealing with various issues in their lives and they all have some types of struggles, either current or from their past. Recall from Chapter 1, they are the walking wounded. They are scarred by their experiences in life that may be too many to list. Is this the tribe I want to belong to? I certainly have my own wounds. Is this the wounded tribe of people Jesus sought?

We all want to belong to a tribe. Some of us find it within our family. Others find belonging through a hobby group, Rotary Club, friends at our job, or even a bar. Our need to belong is often fulfilled by participating in multiple groups. In the church we choose as our tribe, we want to fit in with the group. We want to feel comfortable. We feel this comfort when we believe that others have compatible thoughts, beliefs, and values as they relate to our faith. There is a need to be on the same page when it comes to God. When members of our tribe start thinking or believing something that is difficult for us to accept it creates anxiety, if not outright conflict. How homogenous must we be? How much diversity in the tribe can we tolerate? What did Jesus tolerate and what did he not tolerate?

WRESTLING QUESTIONS

Tribe

1. Where do you fulfill your need to belong?

2. A flock of geese, a rafter of turkeys, a covey of quail, a murder of ravens: who is your tribe?

3. How does your church make people feel welcome?

4. How do you make people feel welcome?

5. Does it make a difference to consider everyone "the walking wounded"?

6. How tolerant are you of people different than you? Can you sit in a pew with a goose on one side and a raven on the other?

7. What would it take to make you consider leaving your church tribe?

GOD'S NATURE

The story in Genesis 32:22-32 tells of Jacob's experience wrestling with God. Since Jacob was left alone that night, there were no witnesses other than Jacob and the man he wrestled with. Near daybreak, Jacob would not let the man go until he blessed him. The man blessed him, renamed him "Israel," and wounded his hip. Jacob spiritually knew that he was wrestling with God. This story has long puzzled me. It seems almost irrelevant to the big picture of Old Testament history. I also question how a mere mortal man could dare to wrestle with his omnipotent creator. I dare not think that I could wrestle with God. However, I do want to learn all about Him.

The Bible is our best source to learn and discover the nature of God. While this statement is true, the nature of God is confusing. My experience so far is that I will never fully understand the nature of God. Most of the Bible presents God as omnipotent (all powerful), omniscient (all knowing), omnipresent (everywhere all the time), loving, merciful, patient, generous, righteous, kind, etc. However, there is also some frightening stuff that seems contradictory to the good stuff.

When God was giving instructions to the Hebrew people about how they were to conquer the land he had promised to their forefathers, he instructed them to kill all the inhabitants of the land; men, women, children, and even their livestock. (Deuteronomy 13:12-15). Led by Joshua, that is exactly what the Hebrews did when they attacked Jericho. They killed all the men and women, young and old, and their cattle, sheep, and donkeys. (Joshua 6:20-21). Take no prisoners. The only exception was Rahab and her family because she had sheltered Hebrew spies. Sounds brutal, doesn't it? We understand that God's purpose was to protect the Hebrews from the wicked ways of the people they were conquering. God did not want them to chase after the false gods of the land and adopt their evil religious practices. The Hebrews were weak spiritually and God knew they would be vulnerable.

God had a master plan. He wanted to groom his chosen people for the coming of a Messiah that would save the world. Prophets predicted this and Jesus became the fulfillment of the prophecies as we move from the Old Testament to the New Testament. God was creating a new covenant with not only his chosen people, but to the whole world. Jesus was the living embodiment of that new covenant. In him, we see the clearest picture of God the Father. Jesus answered: "Don't you know me, Phillip, even after I have been among you such a long time?

Anyone who has seen me has seen the Father. How can you say, 'Show us the Father'." (John 14:9). This brings up an important question: Have you wrestled with the concept of the Trinity?

We serve a triune God; Father, Son, and Holy Spirit. As the saying goes, they are one in three and three in one. Some people, like me, find this confusing. Many pastors avoid the topic, perhaps because it is too difficult to come up with a concrete answer. As you just read in the previous paragraph, Jesus' question to Phillip clearly refers to two distinct beings, God the Father and Jesus the Son. Yet, Jesus was telling Phillip that he and the Father are so similar that knowing one creates the path to know the other. There are repeated stories in the gospels where Jesus talks about his Father, goes off privately to pray to his Father and commune with him, and states that he is only doing his Father's will, the one who sent him into this world. Two distinct and separate beings.

If they were only one being, wouldn't it make Jesus seem just a little bit crazy? It seems he would be making statements like, "I am going to go over yonder and pray to myself." Or, "I can only do what I told me to do, not my will, but my will." Sounds a little off, doesn't it? Also, in the creation story and the fall of man, God said, "The man has now become like one of us, knowing good and evil. (Genesis 3:22a). This wording implies that the Godhead is more than one, it is "us."

Yet, Jesus also said, "I and the Father are one." (John 10:30). The Gospel of John starts out in chapter 1 with the New Testament version of the creation story. "In the beginning was the Word, and the Word was with God, and the Word was God. He (Jesus) was with God in the beginning. Through him all things were made; without him nothing was made that has been made." (John 1:1-3). "The Word became flesh and made his dwelling among us. We have seen his glory, the glory of the One and Only, who came from the Father, full of grace and truth." (John 1:14). So, following this scripture, the Word is God. The Word became flesh and dwelt among us. Therefore, Jesus is God.

Still confused? Do not feel alone. One attempt at the Trinity is the analogy using water, which has three forms; solid (ice), liquid (water), and gas (vapor or steam). Each is different, but they are all forms of the same thing.

In his first of three commentaries on the Book of Genesis, *Be Basic*, Warren W. Wiersbe states, "This one true God exists as three Persons: God the Father and God the Son and God the Holy Spirit. This does not mean that one God manifests Himself in three different forms, or that there are three gods; it means that one God exists in three Persons who are equal in their attributes and yet individual and distinct in their offices and ministries. As the Nicene Creed (325 AD) states it, "We believe in one God... And in one Lord Jesus Christ, the Son of God, begotten of the Father, light of light, very God of very God, begotten, not made, being of one substance with the Father... And the Holy Ghost." For those of us wanting to go deeper, the entire first chapter of this book is a good treatise of the topic.

Acknowledging my own limitations, I must consider

them to be three separate beings, yet three that are inseparably connected. Jesus said, "But at the beginning of creation, God made them male and female. For this reason a man will leave his father and mother and be united to his wife, and the two will become one flesh. So they are no longer two, but one." (Mark 10:6-8). The two are separate, distinct beings, but their marriage binds them together as one entity. In a similar way, the Father, Son, and Holy Spirit are bound together with such perfection, power, and majesty as I can only hope to one day grasp. I am drawn to Wiersbe's line, "...equal in their attributes and yet individual and distinct in their offices and ministries." Jesus' question to Phillip then, makes more sense. If we know Jesus, we know the Father.

Jesus was the perfect example of love, compassion, understanding, and everything we hope for in the way we desire to be treated by our creator. Everything recorded in the gospels points to a loving God, who loves us beyond our ability to fully understand it. But anyone who does not love does not know God, for God is love (1 John 4:8). We are sometimes amazed at how much God loves us, and we have put our trust in his love. God is love, and all who live in love live in God and God lives in them. (1 John 4:16). 1 Corinthians 13 is known as the love chapter, a beautiful presentation on the importance and centrality of love. We are loved beyond our limited ability to fully grasp it.

One might think Jesus was just a meek, mild, and mellow guy. Not so. He spoke with great passion and could be driven to anger. He blasted the religious leaders of his day for becoming a wedge between the people and God. They heaped rules and duties on them while living a life of privilege. (Matthew 23: 1-36). Jesus drove the money changers from the temple, turning over tables, and accusing them of defiling God's house (Matthew 21:12). Both stories of righteous anger are totally reasonable and easy to accept.

But there is one story about Jesus that frightens me; the story of the fig tree. Jesus was hungry and approached the fig tree for fruit. Being out of season, the fig tree had none. Jesus cursed it and when he and the disciples passed by the tree the next day, it was dead. (See Mark 11:12-21). Wow! God's wrath is quick and sure. Explanations of this passage point towards the power of prayer and a warning for us to be fruitful in our faith. If Jesus was trying to teach his disciples a lesson, it seems like he could have conveyed his message another way. I have not read an explanation that fully alleviates my fear. Looks like I will have to continue wrestling with this one for now.

WRESTLING QUESTIONS

God's Nature

1. When you think of God, what image comes to your mind?

2. Is God aloof and distant, or is he up close and personal?

3. Is God righteous, just, and fair?

4. Is God ever unfair or mean?

5. What is your understanding of the Trinity: Father, Son, and Holy Spirit?

6. If you believe that your sins are forgiven and forgotten, should you still fear judgement?

7. How do you see your relationship with God? Is it developing?

GRACE

Grace is the unmerited favor of God. (Ephesians 4:4-9, John 1:16). Why should God, the creator of the universe, take an interest in you? It seems like He would have better things to do. Yet, He is interested. In fact, He knows everything about you. Even the hair on your head is numbered (Luke 12:7). To top that off, He likes you. He hangs in there with you moment after moment, day after day, year after year, for your entire life! His patience is beyond comprehension. His love for you is off the charts. The Creator of the universe wants to have a personal relationship with you! I suspect most of us don't really believe this, yet it is true.

Why am I so important to God? How can that be? Part of the answer lies in the fact that we were created in His image. We are not Him, but we bear a slight resemblance. That resemblance grows as we follow and integrate those principles and things that He taught us. Then, we really do become more like Him, and we more closely represent His image. This is what He wants, to draw us closer to Him and for us to integrate His teachings into the person we are becoming. We do not lose our individuality. We each were created as one-of-a-kind. As we individually grow in our faith, we become the unique person we were designed to be, a one-of-a-kind creation of someone closely connected to Him.

Wherein lies that close connection? It is the bond of love. His love for us is overwhelming, beyond our ability to fully understand it. His love is the foundation of our relationship. Because of His love, grace abounds. We receive this incredible love from God, and we did nothing to deserve it. In fact, we cannot do anything to deserve or earn it. It is given freely.

Yet, in our earthly experience, nothing is free. When we experience God's love, we naturally want more. So, what can I do to get more of God's love? One might mistakenly assume that we need to work for it, that in realty it is not "free". I will pray more. I will do more good deeds for others. Yes, I will be an unstoppable servant to others. I will read my Bible more. I will put my brain in check when some impure thought enters in. Then, God will love me more and bless me with more love. This worldly thinking misses the true meaning of grace.

Jesus said, "Come to me all of you who work and are heavy laden, for my yoke is easy. I will give you rest." (Matthew 11:28-30). Really? I do not have to do anything? Hard to imagine. I can find my spiritual rest in Him without having to earn it or pay for it. Wow! My heart wants to love Him back. Though it is not a require-ment, I then want to do things for Him, to serve Him, to do His will out of gratitude and thanksgiving. This is the effect grace has on us. Amazing Grace, how sweet the sound!

Many of us have heard that grace is getting what we do not deserve and mercy is not getting what we do deserve. Those of us courageous enough to be truly honest with ourselves know that we have very good reason to appreciate mercy. We feel a tremendous relief. Whew! I certainly got off the hook without paying the price on that one! Have you ever been pulled over by a police officer and given a warning instead of a ticket? Ever play Monopoly, happy to get that get out of jail free card? That is mercy.

Grace goes beyond mercy. After the get out of jail free card, after the policeman's warning, then what? We are saved by grace. This grace comes to us through the death of Jesus Christ and does for us that which we cannot do for ourselves. With mercy only, being let off the hook, we are left floating out there on the sea, uncon-nected. Grace lands us into a connection with God that moves us forward in purpose and meaning. Grace is that anchor that keeps us from drifting. Grace is freely given.

I believe that most of us do not get it. I include myself. At best, we comprehend only an occasional glimpse at the amazing depth of grace. If we fully under-stood the totality of the unmerited favor of God, each of us would live our lives very differently. As the moon wanes and waxes, politics would wane and serving others would wax. Bitterness would wane while love and compassion wax. Conflict between Christian denominations would fade away. War would become a dark spot, existing only in the past, where there is no moon at all. Perhaps we will not fully understand until we die and pass on to the next life.

In his book, *Life After Life*, Dr Raymond A. Moody, Jr. began to see a similarity in the stories told by patients who had been clinically dead and then revived. He began a study to record their experiences and capture the commonalities, as well as some differences. As a doctor, he attempted to remain objective and true to the medical model, avoiding religion. His reluctance to interject his own opinions gave his work even more credibility. There have been many books since then on the topic, but his work had the greatest impact on me as a young enthusiastic follower of the Way.

The story might have gone something like this. At your moment of greatest stress and pain, you felt yourself going out of your body. You might have found yourself hovering over your crumpled body in what used to be a car, or looking down at the operating table where doctors and nurses were frantically trying to bring you back. You then experienced going through a tunnel where you could see a light on the other side. Upon arrival, you were greeted by a "being of light," brighter than any light you had ever seen. You were drawn to the light, feeling love, peace, and an overall sense of goodness. The light spoke with you, not in words, but with direct thoughts.

The light reviewed your entire life with you in great

detail and extremely fast. When you screwed up, when you went through dark times, the light did not condemn you. When you judged yourself harshly, the light said that you were learning. You wanted to stay with the light, but were told that you needed to go back. You had more work to do, more to accomplish before you came back permanently. Some might be given the choice as to whether they wanted to stay or return for some special reason. Perhaps the most compelling part of the story is that the light was completely pure in every way. Most of all, pure love.

Though there is nothing in scripture that addresses this, there is a truth here that has captured me. I believe that the light is The Light; Jesus. As much as I respect Dr. Moody's attempt at objectivity, I am drawn to the belief that what those people commonly reported was an encounter with Jesus.

Maybe this is the real judgement day. A day filled with grace and truth. Perhaps it happens for each of us upon our passing from this earthly life. When I stand in front of The Light, Jesus, and experience His pure love, pure grace, pure mercy, and pure forgiveness, how could I experience anything other than pure joy and happiness? How could I have any response but to love Him back? Do I deserve it? No. Did I earn it? No. Yet, I receive it. I am overcome with humility and thanksgiving.

This is the God I am drawn to, the One who loves me. The One I will worship and follow for eternity.

WRESTLING QUETIONS

Grace

1. Do you believe that God loves you? If so, how much?

2. Are we worthy of his love?

3. Have you struggled with the Old Testament harshness of God as compared to the New Testament love of God? How can we reconcile this?

4. Did the Old Testament reveal God to be a loving God, as well?

5. As you have been given grace, can you become better at extending grace to others?

6. What do you believe about "Judgment Day"?

CALLING

What is my calling? What does God want me to do as a servant in His kingdom? Have you ever wrestled with that one?

Many of us are aware of the great commission: Then Jesus came to them and said, "All authority in heaven and on earth has been given to me. Therefore go and make disciples of all nations, baptizing them in the name of the Father and of the Son and of the Holy Spirit, and teaching them to obey everything that I have commanded you. And surely I am with you always, to the very end of the age." (Matthew 28:18-19). But few of us have any idea of how to do that and most of us feel poorly equipped with the skills needed.

1 Corinthians Chapter 12 talks about gifts of the Spirit. Gifts start with Apostles, then move on to prophets, teachers, workers of miracles, healers, helpers, administrators, and those who can speak in different tongues (languages). Of course, we know that the

greatest gift is love, so eloquently and poetically presented in the following chapter. As parts of the body, the church, we all have been blessed by the Spirit with some gifts of one type or another that can be used to further the church and contribute to the great commission. The problem is that many of us have a difficult time trying to figure out which gifts we can claim as our own.

In a church we attended many years ago, the church leadership took on the challenge to help everyone in the congregation discover their gifts and talents. We spent about two years in self inventories, discussion groups, support groups, and sermons dedicated to the topic. At the end of that time, we had not gained any traction in moving forward. We were, in effect, about where we had started. What went wrong?

In hindsight, which we say is always 20-20, the effort was "me" focused. What are 'my' gifts and 'my' talents? What do 'I' want to do with 'my' abilities? In addition to being "me" focused, the effort lacked a clear mission. No one, including me, saw that the mission had already been given to us in the great commission. Short sighted; downright myopic.

Still, the challenge remains. What are my gifts and talents? Can I be given new abilities? Should I develop new capabilities? Where is my niche in contributing to the great commission? Those of us who largely go unnoticed because of our personalities or by nature of our life situation, such as a job that is not in the category of having high interaction with others, often do not see ourselves as having any talents or gifts. For some, identifying gifts and talents is easy. For others, it is brutally painful.

Perhaps the answer lies in the Great Commandment. "Teacher, which is the greatest commandment in the law?" Jesus replied: "'Love the Lord your God with all your heart and with all your soul and with all your mind.' This is the first and greatest commandment. And the second is like it: 'Love your neighbor as yourself.' All the Law and the Prophets hang on these two commandments." (Matthew 22:36-40). Is it possible that by loving God completely, and then spreading that love to others, that we can further the mission of the church? The Great Commission fulfilled by the Great Commandment?

Remember C.S. Lewis' statement that he, an atheist, was drawn to fellow professors who had something he liked and wanted. He gradually discovered that they were Christians. I am confident that his friends were givers of love, and that they also shared with him the source of their love. So, perhaps we, too, can be love spreaders who further the mission of the church regardless of what gifts and talents we may or may not have.

Going deeper, while we can spread love to strangers, which also matters, the greatest impact we have on others is through relationships. The stronger and deeper the relationship, the greater the impact of building that relationship on a foundation of love. This takes work and can be difficult. We have experienced the good times and bad times of relationships with parents, spouses, and children. In expanding the circle to friends, my church family, and co-workers, similar challenges and blessings happen. Even with a stranger, my mindset and approach to that person can make all the difference in the world.

To be effective as a love spreader, I must start with my first and primary relationship. I must love God with all my heart, soul, and mind. I must also know, with certainty, that He loves me. When I come to even remotely understand the depth of His love, responding back to Him in love is easy and natural. In saying "remotely understand" the depth of His love, I believe that His love is beyond our ability to fully comprehend it. We catch glimpses, and even those glimpses can overwhelm us, fill us, inspire us, and be the source of great joy. With that foundation, I know that I am loved even when I am trying to love someone who is difficult to love or who does not love me back. Challenging? Yes. Impossible? No, even though it sometimes feels that way.

All relationships require work and care, just like taking care of your car. If you never fill the gas tank or get periodic oil changes, it will not last long. But, if you care for it well, it will give you many years of help and service. So, I must attend to my primary relationship with God. This is done through prayer, reading my Bible, fellowship with other Christians, worship, and service. This relationship requires my time and energy. I then must move on to my family, investing the same effort in those relationships as I have in my primary one with God. Going beyond family, I then attend to my broader circle of friends, church, and co-workers. Most of us stop after reaching this point. We have used up our available time and energy.

Is it OK to stop here? Maybe, maybe not. In being a love spreader, have you taught, encouraged, and empowered the people in your circle to also spread love? How about the strangers in your community who have had no one who took the time and energy to spread love to them? As the number of relationships increase in your life, can you keep them all at a deep and personal level, or do some of your relationships become more limited? Perhaps you can find a mentor or coach, someone that you trust and someone who can guide you along the way. Someone may seek you out to be their mentor.

So, in all your relationships, become a love spreader. Do not wait for some gift, talent, or calling to be discovered or dumped on you. Use what you have already got under your belt to go love people.

WRESTLING QUESTIONS

Calling

1. Have you explored your gifts and talents?

2. What are they?

3. Can you find a way to serve God and serve others without having "talents"?

4. Is it difficult to fulfill the Great Commandment? Why?

5. How do we fulfill the Great Commission?

6. Can we fulfill the Great Commission without preaching?

7. What are you going to do about it?

MY STORY

The sport of wrestling was part of the curriculum in physical education class during my freshman year of high school. My circle of friends took the sport off campus and into our homes and yards. Being somewhat smaller than my buddies, I often went home with rug burns or grass stains. Great fun! As time went along, I wrestled with other challenges. Mom was willing to sell me a car, but I needed to get a job to pay for it. If I had a car, I could ask a girl out on a date. By the time I was a senior, I had a car that was paid for and a job. I was on the football team and in a rock band. My grades were good. Busy guy. So, where was I going to go from there? There were bigger issues with which to wrestle.

We were not raised in a home of regular church attenders. My brother, sister, and I were taught Christian principles and the Holy Bible was prominently displayed on our coffee table in the living room, dusted regularly, but never read. If we went to church at all, it was the annual trek for Easter.

I recall pondering the existential question, "Why do I, or any of us, exist?" Are we here just to eat, survive, reproduce, and die? Or, is there some greater purpose to existence? Though I found no answer, I found myself drawn to the idea of helping troubled youth to grow up to have successful and productive lives. I chose Psychology as my major for an undergraduate degree.

While in college, I remember a discussion with my brother, who was six years my senior. As a liberal college intellect, I put forth the notion that everything is relative, that there was no absolute truth. He asserted that there was an absolute truth, that he knew what it was, but declined to tell me. When I challenged him on his assertion, he stated, "You are not ready for it yet." This greatly irritated me. I found it arrogant and condescending. I would later come to realize that he made that statement because he had found his faith in God, and knew that absolute truth existed. He also could see that I was not yet through the cycle of higher education mental gymnastics.

After college, a recession hit the economy and jobs were hard to get. I applied all over the state for county jobs as a probation officer or social worker. I sent out many applications and went to multiple job interviews where fifty people were applying for one or two openings. The most common feedback I received was to get some experience under my belt. I was competing with people who had plenty of it.

I soon took a position at a private correctional facility for boys with behavioral and emotional problems. Each Sunday, the youth had to attend a "voluntary attendance non-denominational church service" that was always led by the same Baptist preacher. My job was to supervise the boys during the service and make sure there were no disruptions. As the weeks went by, I could not help but listen to the messages brought each Sunday. Slowly, I began to think that this might be for me, too. Perhaps this was the answer to that vacant space, that longing place, that exists in each of us. Perhaps this was the answer to my existential question.

My need for THE answer grew, and my sense of needing to do something about it increased. I could not talk about it with anyone, not even my adorable wife. It was a private battle. Then, while driving to pick up a fellow employee on our way to work, I said something to the effect of, "OK, God, if this is how it is supposed to work, please forgive me for my sins. I come to you with my burdens. I want you to become the Lord and Master of my life, I surrender my will to yours, and I will follow you."

A flood of something came over my body, from the top of my head on down. I felt tremendous relief, peace, and joy. I started weeping as I was driving down the road. I felt so thankful. (I later came to believe that this flood was the Holy Spirit entering me and making His presence known). The tears would not stop flowing. I felt unconditional, overwhelming love. I knew that I had to get my act together before I picked up my coworker. He would think I was nuts.

For weeks, I could not talk about it. My acceptance of Jesus as my Lord was so raw and personal that I could barely think about it without starting to cry. I finally shared my experience with my wife, who surprisingly seemed happy to hear of this change in her husband. She had wanted to start going back to church, something we had not done in our young married life. She wanted our daughter to grow up in a church family.

"Aha!" Everything began to click and make sense. The existential question, "Why are we here?" was becoming clearer. God, the creator of the universe, created each one of us. We are put here on this planet to learn many things and many lessons, which we take into eternity. Our pain, our struggles, our joys, and the knowledge we gain are all paths to a life of purpose and meaning. We choose our response to life. My brother was right; there is an absolute truth. It is just that none of us will ever fully grasp the whole truth. Just because I could not see the whole truth did not mean that absolute truth did not exist. What we now see only in part, someday we will see fully. (1 Corinthians 13:12).

I was twenty-three when I accepted Jesus as my Lord and Savior. In the many years that have followed, I have continued to develop my faith, my knowledge of scripture, my understanding of life, my relationships with others, my understanding of myself, and, most of all, my relationship with Him. Some of my lessons have been painful, taking two steps forward and three steps back.

Some experiences have been wonderful and my blessings have been beyond my imagination and beyond what I deserve. Grace abounds.

I am not the same person I was at the age of twenty-three. As a young man, life was mostly all about me. As time has passed, I have learned that it is not about me at all. It is about the wonderful creation in which we are lucky enough to live and belong. It is about learning to be in relationship with others and God. Most of all, it is about the fabulous creator who made it all happen. Yet, after all these years, I still find myself wrestling with various issues, with not having all the answers. With many things, I have accepted that I will never fully understand them in this temporal life. Most likely, no one can.

WRESTLING QUESTIONS

My Story

1. What is your story?

2. Have you found God in your life, or has God found you?

3. Are you still searching for the spiritual part of your life?

4. If you are a Christian, how has following Jesus changed you?

5. Do you feel that your life has been "transformed"? (Romans 12:2)

ACKNOWLEDGMENTS

I owe much to my parents, especially my mother, Louise, whose integrity, courage, and example has deeply impacted me and generations yet to come. The depth of her love for others was a clear reflection of the lord of her life, Jesus.

To my wife, Denice, that she continues to lead a life of service and love. She has tolerated my shortcomings for over fifty years, and is the wind that has allowed me to fly. She has helped to pick me up on those occasions when I have crashed. She has always spoken openly and from the heart in our morning coffee conversations.

To my children and their spouses, solid rocks that bring great joy to their parents. I take great pride and affection with them all. At times, they are now my teachers, and I cherish our relationships.

And, I must express a special acknowledgment to my daughter-in-law, Autumn Lindsey, for her support and help in guiding me through the publishing process, editing, artwork, and solid advice. She and my son, Peter, provided ample theological fodder during morning commutes over a period of several months while working on their house.

I have been blessed with church friends, too many to list individually, for their depth of insight in Bible studies and growth classes.

A great debt of gratitude is extended to some ordained ministers I have known over the years. Their influence has helped me through their example, teaching, faith, witness, and compassion. There is no way to scale the value of their unique influences, so by their age:

Dr. Kenneth Heflin, retired Methodist Pastor

Dr. Robert Smith, Professor Emeritus at Point Loma University

Dr. Mark Lehman, District Superintendent, SW OK District, Nazarene Church

Pastor Darlene Franks, Church of the Nazarene, Oroville CA

Pastor Matthew Garner, Church of the Nazarene, Sutter Creek CA

Pastor Austin Bender, Church of the Nazarene, Sutter Creek CA

Most of all, I thank God, whose prevenient grace drew me nearer to Him while I was yet clueless. The "still, small voice" of His Spirit beckoned me to come to Him not out of fear, but out of love. He guides my thoughts and actions still, never forcing His will. I am given the choice to listen and obey, or ignore and rebel. When I obey that which He has taught us, I enjoy a right relationship with Him. When I rebel, His love and patience is not taken from me. He waits for my return. I have the assurance of standing before the throne of eternity and being welcomed, not condemned. I have an advocate, Jesus Christ, who will stand up for me and claim me as His own.

RECOMMENDED READING

The Bible, a combination of sixty-six books written by multiple authors. I prefer the New International Version, but any version that the reader is comfortable with is fine. For people new to the Bible, an introductory class is advisable to help put the stories in perspective. Perhaps one of the New Testament Gospels is a good place to start. Reading and studying the Bible is a life-long adventure.

Mere Christianity, C.S. Lewis, 1952, HarperCollins Publishers. This book is one of the best treatises on the Christian religion. It is not an easy read, but a great one.

Life After Life, Raymond A. Moody, Jr., M.D., 1975, Mockingbird Books. Though Dr. Moody's research is not biblical, his findings provide a convincing case for life continuing after one leaves the earthly body.

When Bad Things Happen to Good People, Harold S. Kushner, 1981, Avon Books. Rabbi Kushner provides a comforting presentation of how people can continue to connect with God in the face of the unfair tragedies we experience in life.

ABOUT THE AUTHOR

Stephen Lindsey and his wife, Denice live in the historic gold mining foothills of the Sierra mountains in California. Their three adult children have blessed them with ten grandchildren and three great-grandchildren.

Stephen holds a Master's Degree in Social Science from Azusa Pacific College. He has worked in residential treatment foster care and the semiconductor industry. He has taught adult Christian Education classes for over forty years.

He has a passion for music and plays piano and guitar. One of his great joys is playing piano in the church Praise Band. Many of his original compositions have been published. He and Denice enjoy hiking mountain trails and exploring the wonders of God's creation. They also enjoy traveling to the wonderful places on earth that we are all drawn to because of their beauty and inspiration.

Printed in June 2023
by Rotomail Italia S.p.A., Vignate (MI) - Italy